10636

B
Bec
Beckerman, Emma
No ████████ go

1. All members of the Congregation and their families are entitled to use the library and draw books.
2. Reference books, such as encyclopedias and dictionaries, are to be used only in the library.
3. All other books may be retained for two weeks.
4. Two cents a day is charged for each book kept overtime.
5. Injury to books beyond reasonable wear and all losses shall be paid for.
6. No books may be taken from the library without being charged out.

DATE DUE

NOT SO LONG AGO

A RECOLLECTION

by

EMMA BECKERMAN

Bloch Publishing Company
New York

Table of Contents

With thanks to the family who were so helpful and involved in this creation, and especially to Michael, without whom this book would not have been written.

Forward

I was born in 1898, in a small Austrian town where persecution and segregation of the Jews was commonplace. Because my father could not find work, we emigrated to Hannover, Germany when I was eighteen months old. For two years, my parents struggled with an even more vicious discrimination, and then decided to emigrate to America in 1904. Could I have forseen the future I would have blessed that cruel oppression; it saved our lives, for we were already in America when Hitler came to power some years later.

When I was twenty-five, I married a truly good man, a member of the newly-formed Amalgamated Clothing Workers Union. He was a great believer in continuing education, and worked to raise the standard of living of all people-men and women-regardless of race, color or creed. To him I dedicate the episode, "School Is For Always". Our son and daughter inherited his implicit faith in the value of education and impressed its importance on our six grandchildren.

Encouraged by my husband, I, too, benefited from continuing my education. I had a radio program called "Poetry by Emily White", on which I read the poems of many authors. I took courses at night while I was working, and was finally able to get out of office management which I detested, although it payed handsomely. My husband died when I was forty-eight; at fifty, I became a dietician, working at the Workman's Circle Home for the Aged as the head of dietetics, a job I loved.

Of course, there were hard times. But looking back, seeing my son and daughter, six grandchildren, and now two great-grandchildren, I can truthfully say, "It's a great life."

Papa Leaves for the Golden Land

I SPENT my first sleepless night when I was four, at the turn of the century. It must have been quite late when I awoke and heard hushed voices in the kitchen. Mama was weeping. As I made my way there I heard her say, "It's a mistake to give up so soon. In three months, after the baby is born, I'll get some work to help you."

"And have eveyone say I can't make a living for my family?" Papa asked. "It *was* a mistake, but we made it two years ago coming to Hannover. We should have gone straight to New York from Austria. Here they have work only for those blond Germans, not me." He pointed to his bristling black beard. "I'd better leave while there's still enough steerage money for me and something left for you until I get work."

"Papa, don't go away, don't go away," I cried.

Mama turned quickly, "I thought you were asleep, Emmy."

"I want Papa to stay with us."

Mama patted my head. "Go back to sleep. We'll talk about it in the morning."

At breakfast, Mama's eyes were red and Papa's face looked different.

"Emmy," he said, seating me on his knee, "you must know that I don't want to leave Mama and little Freddie and you. But it's not good here. I'll send for you as soon as I get a job. It won't be long, you'll see." His glance included Mama.

Things did work out. Several months later my sister was born. She was the only one who inherited Mama's milky-white skin and golden hair. Mama promptly named her Goldie. Soon what little money Papa had left was gone. Mama found a part-time job selling paste jewelry door to door. A neighbor's fifteen-year-old daughter took care of us.

Every evening Freddie and I asked eagerly, "A letter from Papa?" When there was one, Mama read it to us. At first the letters were cheerful; gradually they became less hopeful.

"Jobs are scarce," he wrote. "There are more jobs for women than men!"

"I need experience, and the bosses don't want to break anyone in."

He was living with Mama's sister Sarah and her husband Max. They owned a bakery where Papa helped with the chores in payment of board. Sarah wrote that Max and his friends had tried to find a job for Papa but nobody wanted to take on a 'learner' who refused to work on the Sabbath. He could not be budged from his conviction that the Sabbath was for prayer and rest.

For Mama, however, things were better. She spoke German without a trace of accent, her fair hair and complexion helped her pass as a native. Working on commission, she was able to pick the late afternoon and evening hours. Every pfennig was saved for the longed-for day when we could join Papa.

"If things go on as they are now, we may be able to go to America in about six months. We may even be able to go second class, not steerage." Her eyes lit up. "And we'll bring Papa a present of one hundred American dollars!"

But this was not to be. Mama turned her ankle and had to stay home several weeks. Freddie got the measles, but it was I who was responsible for the greatest set-back.

Mama told me to take care of Freddie, then three, and Goldie who was a year old, while she went to the grocery. I was five at the time. We played at the table, Freddie and I; Goldie sat next to us in a high-chair. Somehow she slipped and fell. In a panic, I pulled her up, not noticing the little foot twisted around the table leg. She was shrieking when Mama came in.

"She fell, and I picked her up," I explained. Mama lifted her. To my great relief she stopped shrieking. I didn't realize she was unconscious.

With Goldie in her arms, Mama ran to the hospital a short distance away. Goldie's leg was broken in two places.

I didn't get a beating. "Just remember," Mama told me, "if Goldie is crippled, you are to blame."

"It wasn't my fault," I sobbed. "The chair strap was loose."

Mama turned away. "You will not see your sister till she comes home." At that time hospitals permitted children to visit relatives. Often I waited outside while Mama and Freddie went up to see her. How I wished Mama had beaten me!

Goldie was in the hospital for two months. When I asked how she was, I got no answer. Mama rarely spoke to me. When Goldie finally came home, I was not allowed to go near her. However, she made a rapid recovery. Soon she was running about without a sign of a limp. The ban was lifted. Mama spoke to me again. I was happy until I heard her tell a neighbor:

"That stupid child delayed our going to America for many months."

But go we did, and sooner than expected. Things had become too much for Mama. We went by steerage, and brought only a fifty dollar gift for Papa. This was my fault too. But that's another story.

That Stupid Child

I WAS not quite six when I wrecked Mama's carefully laid plan to stay in Germany until she accumulated enough money for us to go to New York. She told us one evening:

"...and not by steerage, we'll go second class and bring Papa a wonderful present, one hundred American dollars."

She was doing rather well selling paste jewelry door-to-door in that small, quiet city of Hannover; quiet, that is, until the disappearance of seven year old Elsa Kassel. Parents were terrified and for some weeks refused to let their children out of the house. Finally, Mama reluctantly gave me and my four year old brother permission to play at the front door. I overheard her whisper to a friend that the police had looked in all the cellars.

"It's silly to look in cellars," I told her. "Elsa must have run away with the gypsies, just like in the story book."

"There are no gypsies here," Mama answered. "Hannover is an orderly place, the police wouldn't let them stay."

She buttoned Freddie's coat. "Take good care of your brother." She tried to button mine, but I drew back.

"I can do it myself."

"Yes, you're a big girl, Emmy. But remember what I told you. Don't talk to strangers. Don't go anywhere with them. Don't take anything from them. Terrible things can happen to children."

We were half-way down the stairs. "Yes Mama," I called back.

Freddie and I took turns jumping rope. It was fun for a while. A few doors away some children were playing house, dividing candy and crackers. Freddie wanted to join them, but I held him back.

"They don't want us. We're not like them. We are strangers here."

"I want some candy." he cried.

"Mama said she has no money for such things," I told him.

"I want candy...I want candy," he screamed.

"So he wants candy," a man's voice said. "Is he your brother?"

I looked up. A tall, blond man was smiling down on us. He looked very nice.

"I'll give you twenty-five pfennig if you'll take this letter to my friend." He held out an envelope.

"Twenty-five pfennig! What a lot of candy that would buy." Slowly I shook my head. "I'm taking care of my brother."

"We can take him along. It's not far." He took my hand.

We walked several blocks. I held on to Freddie. I was beginning to worry. "I won't know the way back," I told the man. His grip tightened. "I'll take you back. We're almost there."

A few blocks further on he stopped before a brick tenement. "I'll wait in the hallway with your brother," he whispered. "Go up two flights and knock on the door. When a man opens, give him the envelope and tell him Uncle sent you. Do you know how to count to two?"

"Oh y-yes," I stammered. I was getting more and more frightened. I climbed those stairs slowly. Such a dark hallway. So many steps. Suddenly I remembered Mama's warning. "Terrible things can happen to children..." I stopped on each step. That man had Freddie. I couldn't go back.

Finally I got to the second floor. Here was the door. Who would open it? My hand reached out to knock; suddenly I pulled it back, ran up the third flight and banged on the door.

A woman answered. I handed her the envelope. "The man told me to give this to Uncle." I sobbed.

"There's no Uncle here."

"He's downstairs with my little brother," I cried. "He said he'd give me twenty-five pfennig."

"Come, let's see the man."

When we got down, Freddie was alone, crying.

"Where's the man?" I asked.

"He said 'that stupid child' and ran away."

The woman took us to the station house and handed the letter to the police. It contained a blank sheet of paper.

I was wrong. Elsa Kassel had not run off with the gypsies. Some time after we came to New York (via steerage) and with only fifty American dollars for Papa, a former neighbor wrote us that Elsa's body was found in a cellar. Whether it was 'Uncle's' cellar we never knew for certain; what was certain was that I was called 'That Stupid Child' for a long time thereafter.

The Gift

MAMA WAS a realist. When she became convinced that her goal to come to America second class and bring Papa one hundred American dollars was not possible, she compromised. The hundred dollars became fifty, and steerage the only alternative. To that end, the teapot was the recipient of every pfennig, the worn bankbook received its few marks weekly.

When we complained about the stale crusts and milk for supper, Mama told us how wonderful it would be to see Papa who is so good and loves us so much.

"A real family we will be again. When we give him the present, he'll be so happy. He'll know that we love him as much as he loves us. That's what we're saving for."

Steerage was a horror; to this day I can feel the smell, the nausea, the crowding and the almost total lack of toilet facilities. Some sixty women and children were herded into the hold of the ship. In most vessels, the hold contained cargo. In this one, we were the cargo.

The crossing was rough; seasick and dizzy, I stayed in

bed. All around me women and children vomited and complained about the food. But food was no problem to me. I couldn't bear to look at it.

"How can they eat, Mama?" I asked. "I feel so sick."

"You'd feel better if you ate. Freddie and Goldie were sick too, but after the first day they ate and now they feel better."

Mama was one of the few unaffected by the heaving and tossing of the vessel. She grimaced as she carefully cut the green spots out of the stale bread and ate it with the soup which looked like sea water.

"You're eating this ... this! Isn't there a better way to go to America?"

"There is. If you hadn't gone off with that man and almost got killed, I could have stayed in Hannover and earned enough money to go in a better ship, second class. Remember?"

I remembered. I was still 'that stupid child'. I turned away and cried.

Mama must have felt sorry. She stroked my hair and offered me a piece of salami, but I pushed it away. She rummaged in her valise and produced a photo.

"You were only four when Papa left. Two years is a long time. Do you remember him, Emmy?"

I looked. Yes, this is my Papa. Deep-set dark eyes and fine features accented by a well-trimmed black beard. "I would know him anywhere, Mama. Anywhere."

"In a few days we'll be together again. Won't it be wonderful?" Her eyes were moist. Suddenly I felt better and reached for the salami.

The trip was finally over, over that is for most passengers. For me, the nightmare lasted a lifetime. Even now I can seldom be persuaded to take the Staten Island

Ferry.

Papa awaited us on Ellis Island. He didn't recognize us until he saw Mama a few steps away. Yes, two years is a long time in the life of a small child. Mama had bought a new outfit for each of us; a bright red dress for me, a pretty pink dress for Goldie, a sailorsuit for Freddie, and a smart gray silk for herself.

"Papa, Papa," we cried. We kissed and laughed and wept.

"It's been so long," Papa said giving me a bearhug. "How you've grown."

Freddie made an effort to push me aside. "It's me, Papa." Papa kissed him and included him in the hug. Goldie shook her blonde curls and pushed her way between us. "Me, too, Papa!"

After a while, we stood back and took a second look. Papa was thinner, his beard a bit shaggy and his suit (the same Sabbath one he had brought from Germany) was faded. He stared at us.

"How well you all look! And such fine, new clothes! How did you manage it, Freda?"

"It was hard at first, going door-to-door with that paste jewelry," Mama answered. "But after a time I got some regular customers and they recommended others. See, I brought you a present, Philip." She handed him an envelope containing five new ten-dollar bills.

"You had all this?" he raged. His face was an angry red. "I had hardly enough to eat. I borrowed from your sister to buy second-hand furniture. You should have sent me the money. Am I not the head of the family?"

Mama was taken aback. "Of course you are," she answered haltingly. "But there wasn't so much money. We have hardly any luggage. There was just enough to buy a new outfit for each of us and bring you this money."

She changed the subject quickly. "Where is Sarah? I thought she would meet us."

"Joey, her youngest, has measles. She couldn't leave the house," Papa answered sharply.

He was silent as he led us through the debris strewn, pushcart lined streets to our new home. Our cold-water railroad flat was on the top floor of a dilapidated four story brick tenement. The stairs and hallways were dark and littered. We had expected so much; going up those four flights, we were bitterly disappointed. 'Is this the golden land?' I wondered.

Papa must have sensed our dejection. His hand shook as he put the key in the lock. The furnishings were worn and shabby. Four rickety chairs, a scarred wooden table, a leaky icebox and a rusty coal stove greeted us. The bedroom contained a sagging double bed and a broken-down bureau. Mama couldn't hide her dismay.

"Couldn't you have borrowed a little more from Sarah?"

"I didn't want to owe too much. If you had sent me the extra money, I would have done better."

"It can't be helped now, I suppose. Where's the bathroom? The children must wash up."

Papa glared. "The toilets are in the yard. They can wash here in the sink." He looked at us, then turned away. His voice broke. "It's the best I could do. A man can't get a good job if he won't work on the Sabbath."

"It's all right," Mama soothed. "Together we'll do better."

That night I was awakened by the sound of angry voices.

"What are you doing with my luggage?" Mama asked.

"I lost my-ugh-collarbutton. I think maybe it fell among your things."

"You don't expect me to believe this," Mama shouted.

"If you must know, I thought you may have forgotten to give me the rest of the money. I'm sure you made more. You said you had such good customers."

I shook with anger. How dared he talk to Mama like that? Was this the same Papa who left us two years ago? We too had been hungry after a supper of day-old bread and milk. Our allowance of a few pfennig had gone to make up that fifty dollars. How Mama had cried over Papa's picture and told us he was the most wonderful Papa in the world. At that moment I hated him.

Suddenly he cried in an agonized voice, "I'm ashamed, Freda. You did so well. This is the best I could do," he kept repeating.

My anger vanished. I was sorry for Papa. So very sorry.

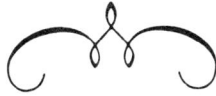

Greenhorn

ALTHOUGH we had been in New York more than a month, I knew only a few 'American' words. However, the word 'Greenhorn' was all too familiar to me. It was usually accompanied by a shove which needed no explanation. It meant 'go away'.

I admired and envied the ease with which Mama made friends. Yiddish speaking neighbors often crowded our small kitchen.

"You haven't been to Orchard Street yet, Freda?" our next door neighbor Mrs. Stein asked.

Mama shook her head. Mrs. Stein's eyes glistened. "You never saw such bargains. Let's go this afternoon."

"Can we come along, Mama? Freddie and I will be so good."

"No, I'll take Goldie with me. You two play outside with Mrs. Stein's daughter Sarah. Don't go away from the door."

"She doesn't want to play with us. She calls us 'Greenhorns'." I looked at our neighbor. "What does it mean?"

Mrs. Stein fidgeted. "It means - eh - people that can't

talk American. I'll tell her to play with you."

But Sarah was in no mood to play with the 'Green-horns'. She soon left us and joined a group of her friends. They danced and sang 'The Farmer in the Dell'.

By the time Mama came home, Freddie and I were in tears.

"Look Emmy, what wonderful things I bought on Orchard Street." She threw the contents of a large paper bag on the table. From a multi-colored batch of materials, she picked up a soiled orange remnant. "I got it for five cents. After it's washed, it will make a nice dress for you."

"Don't you think it would be better if I wore a middy and skirt like the other girls?"

"This is so much prettier. You want to be different, don't you?"

"I want to be just like the other girls. I want to play like them, I want to talk like them, I want to dress like them!"

Mama shook her head. "It sometimes hurts, still it's better to be a little different."

There was no arguing with her, but how I wanted to conform. I wished I were more like her. She *was* different, yet she made friends. A group of women had coffee every afternoon. There was much chatter and laughter. How they enjoyed Mama's stollen. 'The cake,' I thought, 'It must be the cake that makes her so popular'.

That afternoon when Mama sent Freddie and me out to play, I had a piece of the stollen saved from my lunch. Sarah was on the stoop with some friends. They were singing.

"Teach me that song," I begged in Yiddish.

"Go away, Greenhorn."

I showed her the stollen. "You can have it if you teach

me."

She held out her hand. I backed away. "First we sing."

In her loud, nasal voice she sang "My country 'tis of thee.."

"What does it mean?"

Sarah translated. Finally she sang "Land where our fathers died.."

"But your father is alive, and so is mine," I protested.

"You don't understand. Here in America, everybody sings it," she sniffed.

When Papa came home that night, Freddie and I were singing lustily, "Land where our fathers died." Papa didn't understand either. "Maybe you'll learn better next month when school opens."

Bribing Sarah had been a mistake. Now she demanded cake for everything she translated. There just wasn't enough cake to satisfy her. I realized I would have to find new friends. On several occasions Sarah had taken my brother and me to 'Hester Street Park'. It was not far. I took Freddie and went without her.

He pulled at my dress. "There's an empty swing," he shouted. We ran and beat several children to it.

"This is so—so fine," he said. "Swing me high."

On the next swing a little girl tried to compete. "Give me a push," she begged in Yiddish. 'A Greenhorn like me,' I thought. It was nice to talk with another little girl.

"I was very, very sick," she told me. "My stomach hurt so, they took me to the hospital."

"And then what happened?"

"They cut it open and took out my penix. I stayed in the hospital a long time."

"And then?"

"And then I died," she answered.

'How is it here in America people can die and walk and talk like everyone else?' I wondered.

When we tired of the swing, Freddie and I explored the park. A group of children were holding rag dolls and singing. The playground teacher was leading them.

'Put down six and carry two
Tra la la, tra la la..."

I soon parroted the words. Standing a short distance from the group, I joined in loudly. The teacher tried to shoo me away, but I always came back. After a couple of weeks, several of the kids in the chorus came down with the measles and I was admitted to the group. I was told that before vacation ended, we were to perform for everyone in the park.

When rehearsal was over, Freddie and I rushed up the four flights to Mama. I tried to catch my breath.

"Mama," I puffed, "I'm singing with a lot of children in the summer school playground. Soon Mamas and Papas and everybody will come to hear us. Can you make me a rag doll?"

"Why did the teacher pick you? You can't speak English."

"I listened to the words and sang them over and over. And then I stood near and sang real loud. Can you make me a rag doll? They all have them."

"I have some torn socks I should mend. If you're careful not to lose the doll, I'll make you one and take it apart after you're through with it."

I loved that doll with its chalked yellow hair and inky black eyes. I named her Miss Brown in honor of the teacher. How I wished Mama wouldn't take 'Miss Brown' apart after the play. I longed for, yet dreaded the day when Mama and Papa would come to hear me. After that there would be no more Miss Brown, the teacher, or Miss Brown, the doll.

"Why must you take Miss Brown apart? Can't you buy some socks on Orchard Street?"

Mama's eyes were bright. She loved to go to Orchard Street where all sorts of things cost only a few pennies.

"I'll look," she promised. She kept her promise, but at great cost to me. One morning she asked me to mind Freddie and the baby. She didn't return until an hour after rehearsal had started. I tried to tell Miss Brown why I was late, but she understood neither Yiddish nor German. When she waved me away and pointed to the door, I knew I was out of the play. My tears dissolved the yellow chalk on the rag doll's hair.

For the next week, I stood on the outskirts and watched. Two days before the big event, I was out in the rain while the chorus rehearsed. Miss Brown beckoned me inside. She pointed to a place in the chorus. I was so happy, I sobbed out the words.

The big day finally came. I arrived in my new red dress, clutching my Miss Brown.

"I have a surprise," the real Miss Brown was saying. "I bought these dolls for you. You can take them home after the play."

How beautiful the dolls were, each of them different; their hair and dresses in assorted colors. Strangely, Miss Brown handed me one with yellow hair and black eyes. I promptly named her Miss Brown.

'Now there are three Miss Browns,' I thought. The play was a success. Proud parents and friends applauded loud and long. Mama and Mrs. Stein were in the audience. Mama was beaming.

"Look, Mama." I displayed my first real doll. "Miss

Brown said I could keep her."

Mrs. Stein was angry. "I'm going to ask the teacher why my Sarah can't get a doll. She went to summer school too. Come, Sarah."

"I'll go with you," Mama said. "I want to thank the teacher."

We pushed through the crowd surrounding Miss Brown.

"Why didn't my Sarah get a doll?" Mrs. Stein asked angrily. "She went to summer school too."

"She wasn't in the chorus," Miss Brown answered. "I paid for the dolls myself," she added shortly.

"Thank you, thank you," Mama said.

I dragged my feet going home. "I wish you wouldn't take this Miss Brown apart Mama," I begged, hugging the rag doll.

Mama smiled. "I too have a surprise for you." She lifted an assortment of socks. "I bought them on Orchard Street. You can have both Miss Browns."

She smoothed the pink satin dress of Miss Brown the third. "I don't think Sarah will call you Greenhorn any more."

Greenhorn—it left its mark. Even after I learned the language, the sting remained. It was many years before I could admit I was foreign-born.

The Lesson

I LOOKED forward to, yet dreaded, that first day at school. Though it was two months since we left Germany, I hardly understood a word of English, except of course, 'Greenhorn' which was usually accompanied with a yank of my braids. How I longed to speak the language, yet what I learned in school was most rewarding; I learned much more than English.

"I'm so afraid," I said to Mama. "Please come to school with me."

"You know I can't come. The baby is sick. Mrs. Stein's daughter Sarah will take you. All the other children start school at six. You're the right age, you'll make friends there."

She stroked my hair. "See, I made you a nice dress and such a pretty sash."

The dress was bright green, the sash crimson.

"Do girls wear dresses like this to school?"

"Mrs. Stein says it's nice. Better get ready, Sarah will be here soon."

Sarah was unwilling, but Mama's two pennies persuaded her. She was seven and had long, black braids which swung arrogantly as she talked in Yiddish to the 'Greenhorn'.

"Move faster. We'll be late for school." When I hung back, she gripped my hand and fairly dragged me. With a final push, she deposited me in the school yard where the new admissions were gathered.

It was after ten when I got to the classroom. Miss Samuels, the teacher, was at the blackboard. She was tall, her dark hair in a stylish pompador. She wore a white blouse and black skirt. I looked around. Nearly all the children wore middies and dark, pleated skirts. My face soon matched that bright red sash. I shook as I gave her the card. She pointed to an empty seat in the last row.

"Take your seat."

Bewildered, I just stood and looked. Miss Samuels put an arm around my shoulders and led me to the seat. I felt better and smiled as I looked up at her. She said something to a girl in the next row. The girl brought over a pencil and a sheet of paper.

"Say paper."

"P-paper," I stammered.

She did the same with the pencil and seat, then made a sitting motion.

"Paper, pencil, seat," I repeated. The class tittered.

I was in a daze the rest of the day. I heard words and strove to understand. I wondered whether I would ever learn, whether I would ever be like the other girls. I was ashamed of my bright green dress and its huge red sash. Clara, the girl in the next seat pulled at the ends and the sash slipped under the seat. I got up to retrieve it. The class laughed.

"Emma," the teacher said. I made a grab for the sash,

tripped and fell with a loud thud. The laughter of the class became even louder. I couldn't wait to get home.

I dried my eyes as I walked up the four flights. Mama mustn't see me cry.

"Well, Emmy, what did you learn today?"

I held up the paper and pencil. "Paper, pencil," I patted the chair, "seat."

Mama laughed and pointed to the bread and butter. "Bread, butter," she said proudly. "Isn't it good to go to school and learn? I'm so happy for you."

I nodded. How could I tell her about the girl next to me and the laughter of the others?

That Clara! She knew I couldn't make myself understood and took delight in torturing me. She pinched and kicked me whenever she was in the mood, and that was often. One morning, as I sat down, she gave me a particularly vicious pinch. I could take it no longer. Suddenly I howled, I kicked, I scratched. Clara tore at my dress, her nails ripped into my arms. Miss Samuels pulled us apart.

"What's the matter," she asked in German. I stopped in the middle of a shriek. For the first time I could tell what happened.

"She pinches me, always she pinches me," I answered in German.

I don't remember what punishment Miss Samuels meted out to Clara; she moved me to a front seat and told me to stay after school. "I couldn't help it," I protested.

"I know," she answered. "I want to help you learn English."

She gave me a playful pinch. "Pinch," she said. We both laughed. She then picked up her coat..."Coat." She pointed to the sailor hat atop her head..."Hat." So it went. "Gloves, dress, shoes."

I kept repeating each word.

"Enough for today, more tomorrow."

When I got home, Mama wanted to know why my dress was torn and my arms scratched.

"I had a fight," I said defiantly. "I'm glad, glad it's torn. Everyone laughs at it. From now on I will wear only middies and skirts to school."

That was a rewarding day. I learned more than words. I now knew I need not put up with bullying and indignities. I had learned to fight.

This happened more than seventy-five years ago. I still remember Miss Samuels, my first friend.

The Debt

MAMA'S ABHORRENCE of debt bordered on obsession.

"I owe no one anything," she often boasted. When times were bad, and they were for us at the turn of the century, she scoured the neighborhood for day-old bread; fish was bought at closing time, when it was almost a give-away; liver and lungs, cheapest of the meats, were chopped, sauteed, pot-roasted, broiled or fried, and stuffed down our protesting throats. And yet, she incurred a debt. I was the cause.

It was more than seventy-five years ago; I was six at the time. We had been in this country some five months. I spoke barely enough English to make myself understood.

My brother Freddie, two years my junior, and I did not miss the scrupulously clean Hannover streets; we loved the freedoom from the strict German discipline. We reveled in the sights, the noise, the dirt and the crowds of the lower East Side. The pushcarts piled high with slightly rotted fruits and vegetables, the peddler hawking his damaged wares 'only such a little tear and so easy to fix' fascinated us.

Papa, who had preceded us to the "golden land" provided a cold water walk-through on the top floor of a shabby four-story tenement on Houston Street. He, a respected student of the Talmud, now operated a foot-pedalled sewing machine; his wages seldom furnishing the bare necessities. In the circumstances, even a slight illness on the part of the breadwinner became a frightening experience; and now we were frightened. Papa lay on a cot in the kitchen, which also served as a bedroom. His eyes were bright with fever, his thin face and hands a grayish yellow.

"Liver trouble," the doctor told us.

"You'll have to go for the medicine," Mama said. "Lindenman's on Rivington Street is cheap and he gives away glasses and dishes. Here's a two-dollar bill. Hold it tight and take good care of the change. It's all I have."

I clutched the bill and ran the short distance to the drugstore. The medicine cost forty-five cents; my small fist gripped the change. I pointed to the shelf containing premiums.

"I will have that orange glass."

"We give only a plain glass when you pay forty-five cents."

"I so want the orange one, please, please..."

"Oh, all right. Here it is."

I skipped out of the drugstore. I had gone only a few steps when a tall man with a moustache took hold of my arm.

"Little girl, this is no way to carry money. I'll wrap it up good for you and put it in the glass."

I handed him the glass and the change. He tore a piece

of newspaper, wrapped up the money and put it in the glass.

I was nearing home when I realized that the glass felt kind of light, and the quarters and nickel did not jingle. I yanked the paper out. The glass was empty. I sat down on the curb and howled. How could I go home? Mama had trusted me with the last two dollars.

A passing neighbor stopped and asked; "Are you lost, Emmy? I'll take you home."

I howled louder. "Look, the glass is empty. The man took the change from the two dollars, all the money we had." I held up the medicine bottle. "Papa's sick."

The neighbor was puzzled. "The man—he put the money in the glass?"

"He wrapped it in paper."

"Now I understand." She found an empty egg crate and stood on it. "Friends," she shouted. A crowd gathered. In half-English, half-Yiddish, she told the story to the accompaniment of my sobs. She held up the medicine and the glass.

Shabbily dressed, shawl-wrapped women opened small purses and poured pennies and nickels into that orange glass. Men in torn sweaters, men in worn shoes, emptied their pockets of small change. Just as quickly as the crowd had gathered, it disappeared.

"Come, Emmy," our neighbor said. "I'll take you home."

I was trembling as I walked up the four flights. 'She doesn't know Mama', I thought.

Mama was at the door, frightened and angry. "Where have you been all this time? What happened?"

It took Mama some time to get the story straight, but when she did, her eyes blazed. "I don't want the money. I won't take charity."

Our neighbor looked stunned. She glanced at the scarred, rickety kitchen table and wooden boxes which supplemented the battered kitchen chairs, and at the gaunt, yellowed man on the cot.

"How can I give the money back? To whom?" Suddenly she brightened. "I'll tell you what. *You* give it back. When someone comes with a pushka to collect for charity, put in what you can, till it is all paid."

Thereafter, Mama never passed by anyone holding a pushka without putting something in. She kept no track of the money, and though the debt was paid over and over, it was never liquidated.

The Saturday Night Bath on Friday

FOR MOST of us who lived on the lower East Side some seventy five years ago, the weekly bath was a problem. Although it was more than six months since we left Germany, we had found no solution. We made do with a daily scrub of our visible parts and a weekly dunking in an over-sized basin. I was almost seven at the time, my brother Freddie, five.

The pushcarts on Orchard Street replaced the austere cleanliness of Hannover's sidewalks and noisy, rubble-filled Hester Street Park contrasted sharply with Friedrichsvald where Kaiser Wilhelm often vacationed. Strangely, we did not miss the orderly, clean-swept streets or the gardens. We enjoyed the pushcarts with their over-ripe fruits and vegetables. The conglomeration of merchandise from squashed bananas to battered toys delighted us. However, we did miss our Hannover six-footed bathtub.

The newly rented cold water walk-through contained a stationary washtub. Proudly Mama showed us the kitchen.

"See, a sink it has, *and* a washtub. Too bad the tub is so small you can't bathe."

The kitchen also served a bedroom, dining room and occasionally, laundry. It boasted a rusty coal stove, a wooden icebox, some rickety chairs, a battered pine table and a cot for me. A large oval basin doubled as wash boiler and baby bath.

On Mondays, Mama would chip coarse naphtha soap into the basin and boil the clothes for hours, turning our kitchen into a kerosene-scented Turkish bath. Except for the baby, all of us used the naphtha soap and smelled of kerosene most of the time.

"Why can't we use the same soap as baby?" I asked. "Everyone says we smell funny."

"A good, clean smell it is," Mama answered, placing the baby soap on a shelf beyond our reach. She cut two pieces from a large bar of naphtha soap. "See, for you a nice piece and one for Freddie. Friday after school you and your brother go to the baths on Allen Street. You're too big for the washtub."

"Why can't I go to the Mikvah with you?" Mama went there Thursday nights and came home very rosy and clean.

"You have to wait till you're ready to marry. Only married women and girls soon to marry go there to bathe and pray."

"Then why can't we go to Tante Becky? Papa bathes there."

"She has four small children; with Papa and Uncle Henry and her makes seven to use the tub. Enough is enough."

"But Mama, I'm afraid of the baths. In school they say it's a shower and it comes from the top."

"So it's a shower, so what's to be afraid of? Look, I'll show you how it is." She took a colander from the shelf above the stove and filled a pot of water.

"Hold your hand in the sink." Slowly she poured the water through the colander and over my hand.

"That's like a shower. Doesn't hurt, huh? And nice, warm water is there."

"But Mama, I'll have to undress, *naked*! They'll all see me."

Mama nodded and smiled. "So that's what you're afraid of. Nobody showers in clothes, Emmy. And noboby will look at you. They are too busy with themselves."

The following Friday, Mama gave me a washcloth, a towel and a piece of the much despised soap. "Where's Freddie?"

Freddie was balancing himself on an edge of the coalbox. "Freddie," Mama yelled.

He turned, lost his balance and fell face down into the coal. "Ow-" he howled.

"God punished you, for you didn't obey Mama when she said not to play with the coals," she scolded.

Black tears flowed over the bleeding scratches. "I didn't know God was hiding in the coalbox," he sobbed.

Mama washed away some of the blood and grime. "Take this towel and soap. Wash good in the shower."

Friday afternoon was a busy time at the Allen Street showers. A line of boys and one of girls extended halfway round the block. The attendant, lanky and harshvoiced, tried to keep the kids from fighting, but no sooner did she settle one scrap when another broke out. Shouts of "Hey, gimme back my towel—" "Dat's *my* soap— she's sneaking in ahead of me," were heard all along the line. A fat, stringy-haired girl in front of me turned and sniffed. 'Must be that stinking soap', I thought, and covered it with the towel. I wasn't quick enough.

> "Eight and eight is sixteen
> Stick your nose in kerosene"

she chanted loudly.

I fought back the tears. 'She mustn't see me cry. Maybe she'll laugh and show the other girls my patched petticoat. Oh, I don't want to undress in front of them'. I clutched the towel and prepared to run away. Suddenly the bathhouse door opened and I was pushed in.

Mama was right. Nobody looked at me. I started undressing. The fat girl had her clothes off. I turned my eyes away but not before I saw the lumps of fat hanging from her thighs. *She* looked funny.

We were warned to get into the shower and scrub quickly as the water would be turned off in ten minutes, but I was still struggling with my shoelaces when the showers were turned on. There were screams "It's too hot, it's too cold." I tore my clothes off, threw them on the bench and entered the shower. Timidly I tested the water with one hand. It was just right. How wonderful it felt!

The grime-covered wall vanished. I was no longer conscious of the rough, concrete floor. I was bathing in the fountain of beautiful Friedrichsvald; water spouted between the stones of the rock garden and jeweled drops hung from its multi-colored flowers. The warm water felt so good, every hair, every inch of my skin responded to its gentle massage.

'When I grow up,' I promised myself, 'I'll have my own shower and bathe in it every day—no, twice a day, yes, even more'.

"She's snitching my sweater," a girl shrieked. Suddenly I was back on Allen Street. I hadn't even begun soaping. Feverishly I applied soap and washrag. The strong naptha cleaned well but not fast enough. Abruptly the water was turned off. I wiped away the remaining grime and suds.

Outside I looked for Freddie. He was not hard to find. "That boy kicked me," he yelled. I turned to look but the boy had disappeared into the crowd!

"Freddie," I whispered. "Let's get back in line and shower again."

"I thought you didn't want to get undressed."

"Nobody looks at you, you ought to know that," I answered.

We waited in separate lines for another hour. When my turn came, the attendant yelled, "Just look at your dirty, wet towel! When will you kids learn that you can't go in twice?"

But learn we did. We practiced using half the towel and by folding it carefully, outwitted the ogre at the door. The very next Friday afternoon, we triumphed. We got in twice!

Books

ALTHOUGH we lived on the lower East Side about two years and could understand and speak English as well as the other children, the memory of being called 'Greenhorn' still hurt. 'Greenhorn' meant going through a period of derision and often physical abuse from the 'in' group. Even years later it kept me from making friends. Books became my friends.

This pleased Mama. To her all books were sacred.

"Papa has his Talmud and his synagogue. That is good. But you must learn from American books too. Mrs. Schwartz's son studied hard and he became a dentist. Some of his friends work in factories, but others are accountants and engineers. His friend Sammy Cohen is a doctor!"

"I love my books, Mama. They are my friends. This is the third time I took *Little Women* from the library. My teacher explains the hard words."

"Still you should have friends. Maybe some girls on the block would like to play with you."

"Oh no, Mama, They are so bad and they fight a lot.

Only yesterday Lily from the ground floor tripped an old lady carrying two bags of groceries. The bags broke and everything fell on the sidewalk. You should have heard the woman curse!"

Mama was incensed at such goings-on. She decided to speak to Lily's mother and urged her friend Mrs. Stein to accompany her.

"You don't know what you're getting into, Freda," Mrs. Stein said. "That woman had fights with nearly all the neighbors and what a foul mouth she has. She works during the day. No one has ever seen her husband." She added in a whisper, "They say he's in jail."

"Poor woman," Mama answered. "I'm sure she doesn't want Lily to do such things."

The following evening, Mama and a reluctant Mrs. Stein went downstairs. I was worried and waited in the hallway. Mama knocked on the door.

"Who is it?" a harsh voice asked.

"We're your neighbors, Mrs. Rubin," Mama answered. The door opened several inches. The woman was an older edition of Lily. Tall, skinny, with stringy brown hair.

"Well, what do you want?"

"We came to ask you to tell Lily not to kick and push old women carrying bundles. Yesterday a woman dropped two paper bags. Her groceries fell all over the sidewalk."

"Did she do this to you?" Mrs. Rubin asked belligerently.

"No but..."

"Then mind your own damn business." She slammed the door shut.

However, as we walked upstairs, we heard loud slaps

and Lily crying, "I won't do it no more."

From that day on I was a marked girl. And I was afraid. I feared fights and usually outran anyone likely to start one. I knew that sooner or later I'd have to stand up and fight Lily. On several occasions she shouted, "Tattletale, I'll get you yet!" Her shout followed me as I outdistanced her and ran into our hallway. I was determined to delay the confrontation as long as possible.

It was not long in coming. As I was walking home from school carrying an armful of books, Lily and three of her friends pounced on me. They grabbed my arms; the books, including my beloved *Little Women* scattered over the sidewalk. Anger such as I had never felt before lent me a strength I didn't know I possessed.

"My *Little Women*!" I shouted. I tore loose and grabbed Lily by the hair. "Leggo!" Lily shrieked. I gripped her hair more tightly.

"I'll fight, I'll fight you all, one at a time. I know you, Rosie, and you, Ruth, and you, Annie. If anything happens to the books, my mother will see the principal."

Open-mouthed, they picked up the books while Lily pounded and scratched my face, but I didn't feel a thing. In a rage, I held Lily's hair with my left hand and punched with my right. Lily shrieked and scratched, trying for my eyes. I ducked and kept on punching. Suddenly Lily went limp and slipped down. I was frightened.

"Take her," I yelled. Two of the girls held Lily up, the other handed me the books.

Mama was startled by my appearance.

"Because you told Mrs. Rubin about Lily, she and her friends made me fight."

Mama put cold compresses on my face and helped me into bed. The following morning there was a loud knock on our door.

"What kind of child do you have?" Mrs. Rubin bellowed. "I had to get a doctor for my Lily last night."

Mama did not answer but motioned her into the bedroom. My eyes were black and blue, my face scratched and swollen.

Mrs Rubin looked at me for a minute, then left without a word.

"It wasn't me I was fighting for, Mama," I sobbed. "It was my books."

"It's all right, Emmy. Sometimes we must fight. Anyway, it's not as bad as it looks. I didn't have to get a doctor for you," Mama said complacently.

Mother's Helper

AT THE AGE of six, my brother Freddie had become a tough East Side kid. During the two years we lived in New York, the strict German discipline had gradually worn off. Freddie made friends, learned to fight and to speak the gutter English of Rivington Street from his peers. I was two years older, and therefore 'in charge'.

"Freddie," I often admonished, "It's not nice to talk that way."

"Aw, all the kids do. I don't wanna be a sissy."

"You'll go to school in a month. The teacher won't like it."

"I'll be careful," he promised.

However, he wasn't careful enough. The day after school opened he came home crying.

"The teacher said you should come to school tomorrow."

"What happened?" Mama asked.

"I spoke to a boy in the next seat. She hit me with a ruler." He held up a hand covered with welts and bleeding knuckles. "I yelled, 'You sonofabitch bastard.'"

"What does that mean?" Mama asked. Neither of us could tell her, but our next-door neighbor could and did.

"We all go to school tomorrow," Mama said grimly as she applied cold compresses to his hand.

Mama woke up early and made us scrub carefully in the combination wash-tub sink.

"We show that uh...teacher we're not slobs."

She wore the one good dress reserved for synagogue and special occasions. Her gleaming bronze hair was arranged in a smooth pompador.

I shrank from the idea of a confrontation between Mama and the teacher. "Why must I come with you?"

"Maybe I'll not understand that bas..." She stopped short, her usually rosy face turned a deeper red.

But Mama didn't need me to interpret. Three words were sufficient.

"He called me a ..." the teacher lowered her voice, "a sonofabitch bastard!"

Mama lifted Freddie's bandaged hand, then looked pointedly at the teacher. "Is that *right?*" She took my hand and we walked out. The teacher was still sputtering as we closed the door behind us.

When Freddie came home, Mama said gently, "Freddie, you know now that you must not talk in class, and to say such things as... (she couldn't bring herself to say it) is wrong."

"I won't say it again," he promised.

This was another promise he didn't keep. One night he had a toothache; his howling kept us all awake. The next morning, Mama fished a dime out of the teapot.

"Emmy, you'll have to take him to the dispensary to get out the tooth. It has a big hole. They take ten cents."

"Why don't you take him, Mama? I'll take care of the

baby."

"You're the oldest and should help me. I helped my Mama carry milk from the farm when I was six."

I could find no answer and dragged the reluctant Freddie through the door.

"I won't go," he yelled. "The tooth don't hurt no more."

I knew I must get him to the dispensary. But how? Suddenly I had an inspiration.

"I'm sure it won't hurt much and the doctor gives you a quarter if you don't scream," I lied.

"A quarter?" Freddie asked in wonder. "It's a lot of money. I'll go."

The gray, shabby anteroom with its backless benches was filled with patients of all ages. Some held handkerchiefs over swollen faces. Children pulled at their mothers' skirts crying, "Come home, the tooth don't hurt no more."

Every few minutes there was a loud shriek from the doctor's office, then a patient came out holding a blood-stained handkerchief. This provoked new wails from the children.

Freddie's eyes were wide with fright. "Come home," he pleaded, "the tooth is better." I gripped his hand.

"You know how it will hurt when we get home. Mama will be so angry. And remember the quarter."

I was so relieved when the dentist finally got the tooth out, I forgot about the quarter. But Freddie didn't. He refused to budge from the chair. "The quarter," he mumbled, through a mouthful of blood. I put a handkerchief over his mouth and dragged him to the door.

He pushed my hand away and shouted at the astonished dentist, "You sonofabitch bastard. I only gave one little scream."

I pulled him to the street and said not a word about bad language. Come to think of it, I still owe Freddie a quarter.

Learning

IT WAS NOT often that Mama and Papa aired their differences before us children. They had few arguments, for there was little time for them. Papa was engrossed with the affairs of the synagogue and the friends he met daily for morning prayers. And for years after we came to New York, it seemed to me that Mama was either pregnant or nursing a new baby. (Five more children were born after we came to America. Three died within a few weeks of birth. My two sisters, Doris and Pearl, survived.) But when they spoke of learning, their differences were fundamental.

Papa was a traditionalist; the Talmud was to him both past and present, the future—heaven.

To Mama, learning was a means of getting ahead, of attaining everything she expected from the 'Golden Land'; it meant a bright, new life for all of us.

"When you go to school, you must study hard," she often told us. "Some day Freddie will be a great man, maybe even a dentist, and you girls could be teachers or marry rich bosses."

She was the practical one who stretched the meager pay Papa brought home by taking her younger sister Rosie and Cousin Anna into our over-crowded four room walk-through. They paid two and a half dollars each for one bedroom and two meals. Papa brought home very little more.

One evening, when Papa mentioned the sheitel, that is, the wig that Mama wouldn't wear, I leaned forward to listen. The subject was a touchy one. Even at nine, I knew Mama would be the winner.

In the early 1900s many orthodox Jewish women on the lower East Side wore wigs. No, not the glamorous ones we see today. Those wigs were designed to mark the women 'married' and make her unattractive to other men. That ill-fitting bundle of hair could make even a pretty woman less than desirable.

"Mrs. Shapiro has a fine, new sheitel," Papa said.

"You should say Mrs. Shapiro, the rebitzen," Mama retorted angrily. "That's what the neighbors call her. You'd think she was married to a Rabbi, not a presser. I bet she's bald, and hasn't a hair to cut." Mama smoothed her shining, bronze hair.

"A good Jewish wife should do as her husband asks," Papa replied.

"Don't tell me I'm not a good Jewish wife, Philip. I kosher meat, I light candles, and six sets of cracked dishes I have; meat dishes, dairy dishes, and parve dishes, and another three sets for Passover. But wear a wig—never!"

A few days later, Mama asked me to bring the egg-crate which served as extra chair, down to the stoop. I looked up in surprise. I had never seen her on the stoop before. The 'rebitzen' and her clique usually crowded the doorway.

"It's the heat," Mama explained. "The tin roof has turned this top floor into an oven."

Downstairs, the 'rebitzen' was holding forth. A woman grudgingly made room for Mama. The crate creaked as she sat down. The 'rebitzen' was annoyed. She carefully adjusted her sheitel and looked pointedly at Mama.

"Some women forget our ways when they come to America." The group tittered agreement.

"Even Mrs. Katz who came here only a few months ago, goes to night school to learn English. Yiddish isn't good enough for her."

"Who's Mrs. Katz?" Mama whispered to her neighbor.

"She lives on the third floor. Keeps only two sets of dishes, says she doesn't need parve!"

"About the school," Mama persisted. "Does it cost much?"

"It costs nothing."

Mama's eyes glistened. "Is it far?"

"No, it's on Hester Street, near the Park."

That September, Mama was the object of derision. The neighbors' laughter accompanied the 'rebitzen's' strident tones.

"Pregnant she is, with a houseful of kids and boarders, and she goes to school. And that nice husband, poor man, she got him to go too. Carries her books like a schoolboy!"

Mama was delighted with the school. "We are having a democracy. The teacher says when you vote you have a choice." So we became a democratic family.

"Shall we get day-old bread with butter, or fresh rolls without?" she asked. "Speak up, everybody, you must vote."

"Shall we have Papa's shoes fixed or get liver and onions for supper?"

We voted for the crusts and milk. The shoes were a must.

When we were put to bed early because there was no more food in the house, our protests were answered by quotations.

"Early to bed and early to rise
Makes a man healthy, wealthy and wise"

When Freddie asked for a penny, he got another quotation:

"A penny saved is a penny earned
A penny spent is a penny burned"

Freddie turned away in disgust. "How can you burn a penny?"

"You're too young now. You'll find out when you grow up," Mama answered with a wry smile.

School had become important; Freddie and I went during the day, Papa and Mama in the evening.

I was in the third grade when Freddie came down with scarlet fever. A sign plastered on our door proclaimed QUARANTINE! It was more than six weeks before I was allowed back into school. Soon after he recovered from scarlet fever, he caught chicken pox, whooping cough and mumps in rapid succession. We were quarantined again and again.

I was worried abut my school work and cried every time Freddie got sick. I must confess, it was more for my sake than for his.

Two weeks before school ended, I was back in class. I

studied far into the night trying to catch up. It was hopeless. Promotion day was my Black Friday.

"Left back, left back," the jeers of my classmates followed me home. My eyes stung with unshed tears. I wouldn't let them see me cry.

Blindly I rushed up the stairs. Papa was laying out his Tallis and Tefillin for the Friday night services.

I threw myself on the cot and wept hysterically.

"I'm so ashamed. I got left back. I'll never, never go to school again."

"You have nothing to be ashamed of. We all know it wasn't your fault." He put an arm around me. "Here, take this before Mama comes home." He handed me a dollar. "Buy yourself something."

"You're giving me a dollar for being left back?"

"No, no. It's for doing your best."

I hugged him. "I'm going to *be* the best. You'll see, Papa, *nobody* is ever going to get better marks than me."

When Mama came home, I gave her the dollar.

"Let's have a party, Mama. We'd all love to have some sauerbraten."

Mama turned the dollar over and over. She suspected it was play money.

"Where'd you get it?"

Papa looked down at his thin-soled shoes.

"I walked, Freda."

'How many miles had Papa walked to save that dollar,' I wondered.

The following Monday, when Mama served the sauerbraten, I couldn't swallow it. Suddenly a nine-year old was no longer a child.

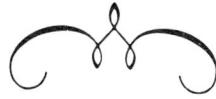

Some Things
You Have to Do

PAPA HAD a hard time finding a job. An Orthodox Jew, he came to New York equipped with a knowledge of the Talmud and a stubborn conviction that the Sabbath must be dedicated to prayer and rest.

When Mama complained that others accepted the ways of this new world, his reply was "Some things you have to do."

His friends tried to make him conform. "This is America," they told him. "Everyone works Saturdays."

Papa stroked his short, black beard. "Some things you have to do."

My brother Freddie and I were often hungry. Sometimes neighbors would give us a few pennies for running errands or minding babies. "Are you sure you earned this money, Emmy?" Mama asked when I gave her my few cents. "You must work for what you get."

I was nine at the time and anxious to help. But it was only after I assured her that I had taken care of a neighbor's baby that she pocketed the money.

One Thursday afternoon, while Mama was making

noodles, an investigator called on us. She was a thin, grim-faced woman in her thirties wearing a dark blue suit and a gray blouse. She asked a lot of questions which Mama answered politely. Mama was accustomed to answering questions; we had been immigrants in Germany.

"What's your name? Your husband's? Where were you born? How long are you in this country?"

Mama continued rolling out the dough. "Excuse me please. It will be too dry if I stop now."

"How long has your husband been out of work?"

Suddenly Mama became suspicious. "Why do you ask?"

"The neighbors say your children are hungry. If you want charity, you must answer."

"Just tell me their names," Mama shouted.

"I can't do that."

Angrily Mama raised the floured rollingpin.

"*I* didn't send for you."

The investigator fled.

"What did she mean, charity?" I asked.

There was a long silence. "We won't talk about it now," she answered finally. "It's something you have to take when there's no other way."

For some time thereafter, Mama eyed each visiting neighbor with suspicion. "My children," she said emphatically, "get plenty to eat; three meals a day and all the bread they want." He blazing eyes dared anyone to contradict her.

The small kitchen was the family gathering place. The furniture consisted of a table, four splintery chairs, a coal stove and an egg crate which served as coal bin. My cot was crowded into a corner. I learned to sleep despite the flickering gaslight, the meal preparation, the family chatter. And there were visitors. On cold winter nights, Mama's sister Rosie and her boy-friend Jake sat near the stove sipping tea and whispering. Jake was a slim, brown-haired boy with friendly gray eyes and a ready smile. He worked in a mattress factory, and although he sometimes complained of the dust, he was glad of the job. He could find no other work; this was 1907, the year of the panic.

Strangely, it was during the height of the panic that Papa found a job. Our neighbor, Mrs. Miller came in one evening greatly excited. Her daughter Sylvia was going back to work. A Mr. Ginsberg had taken over the bankrupt lingerie factory and would hire some new workers.

"It's probably not worth the carfare," Papa said after Mrs. Miller left.

Mama fished a dime out of the teapot. Papa shrugged and took it.

The next afternoon he came home out of breath. He had run up the four flights and could hardly speak.

"I got the job," he finally managed. "At first Mr. Ginsberg didn't want me because I wouldn't work Saturdays, but when I told him how much I needed the job, he said he'd put me on part-time and pay accordingly."

"Accordingly," Papa discovered on payday, was about half the amount per dozen paid the full-time workers. He soon learned to operate the foot-pedalled sewing machine. His smooth, long-fingered hands became adept at joining delicate laces to silks.

On Friday afternoons, he handed Mama his weekly pay envelope. It contained about three dollars. One Friday afternoon he came home in high spirits. "I'm a samplemaker now. I'll get fifteen cents more on the dozen."

Mama was delighted. She put some wood in the stove, took out flour and eggs. That day, for the first time in months, we had a cake.

The following payday however, Papa came home more dejected than ever. He gave Mama $2.65.

"What happened?" she asked.

"The samples take much longer. Each piece is different and has to be perfect. But Mr. Ginsberg said I'll soon get used to it." Poor Papa, he never did make much.

Jake, too, was having trouble. Rosie, hitherto so full of chatter, was silent.

"Why doesn't Jake come anymore?" I asked.

"You mustn't ask questions," Mama interjected.

Rosie suddenly burst into tears. "Jake hasn't been working in months. He's starving. His landslite are making a benefit for him." Landslite (immigrants who came from the same part of the old country) often banded together and made benefits for those even more hard-pressed than themselves.

Mama shook the weeping girl. "Why didn't you tell me? I thought you two had quarreled."

"You had your own troubles," Rosie sobbed.

"Come," Mama said sharply. "Let's bring him here."

Jake was so weak, he had to be helped up the four flights. They put him on my cot in the kitchen.

"I'll make you something good to eat," Mama said. She cut some stale bread into cubes and poured a mixture of hot water and sugar over it. Jake's hand trembled. The food spilled from the spoon. Rosie fed him.

"It's so good," he murmured drowsily. He was asleep in minutes.

When Papa came home, Mama told him about Jake's 'illness'. Papa tried to hide a smile. "So you took in another mouth to feed. And you, always complaining about how little you have."

"Some things you have to do," Mama answered.

Fraidy Cat

THE YEAR was 1910, a time when the lower East Side was infested by gangs, large and small. By small I mean youngsters from six to twelve who tried to emulate the toughness of their senior idols. It was no place for 'fraidy cats', and I was known as one. A thin, awkward twelve-year-old in an era when plumpness was admired, I wore foreign-looking clothes in bright conflicting colors. This made me a target for stones in the summer and snowballs in the winter. Yet even when they chanted 'fraidy cat' my skinny legs outran the young hoodlums. I was determined not to fight except as a last resort.

I blamed all this on Mama's love of color. She was fifty years ahead of her time. She had the eyes of magpie; her sewing basket was a kaleidoscope of orange, purple, crimson, yellow and startling blue.

"Mama, all the girls wear dark blue skirts and white middies," I protested.

"You look very nice," she answered as she tied my purple dress with a yellow sash.

"It's just fine for those little bums to throw muddy

snowballs at," I answered bitterly.

'Those little bums' overturned pushcarts, stole from neighborhood stores and were the bane of small boys and girls. For protection, most children came home from school in groups. I, however, was a loner. The years of being called greenhorn had left their mark. Long after I learned to speak without an accent, I shrank from other children. My bizarre clothes made me feel inferior; I dreaded rejection.

One day Mama brought home a pair of startling blue leggings. I turned away; I didn't want her to see me cry. And I wore those leggings. They became the subject of a composition by the class wit who read aloud:

"And she streaked down the aisle in her electric-blue leggings."

I hid my face in my hands. Above the ensuing laughter, I heard a clear voice say:

"I *like* them." It was Bessie, whose curly brown hair and pink and white complexion I had long envied. Suddenly she seemed the most beautiful girl in the world. I waited for her after school.

"I want to—uh—thank you," I stammered.

"Oh, that composition," she answered.

She gave me a friendly smile. "I told my mother how good you were. Would you like to come to my house and have hot chocolate and cookies?"

I nodded and trudged along. We stopped at one of the newer tenements. It was different from the one we lived in; the hallways were light and clean, the kitchen contained no bed; there were carved oak chairs and a table without splinters. The living room, too, had no bed.

"Where do you sleep?" I blurted out.

"In the bedroom, of course," she answered.

Bessie's mother brought in hot chocolate and cookies. "Do you live nearby?"

"Next block," I mumbled through a mouthful.

"If you and Bessie can do your homework together, it will be better for both of you."

I nodded and suddenly remembered Mama would wonder where I am.

"I must hurry home now. Bessie, can you come to my house Sunday?" Bessie and her mother both said yes.

I rushed up the stairs. "Mama, Bessie will come here Sunday. She has such a grand home."

I was suddenly conscious of my surroundings. I never before noticed our shabby furniture, the much mended clothes strewn over the chairs and beds, the egg crate which stored the coal for the rusty kitchen stove.

"I hope she likes us, Mama. They don't have beds in every room," I added.

Mama's eyes narrowed in anger. "If we're not good enough for her, she's not good enough for us."

I spent the rest of the week cleaning. I tried hard to find a place for the broken toys and raggedy dolls, the frayed sweaters and slippers and underwear, but every drawer and the two small closets were packed solid. Sunday morning I finally gave up and heaped everything on the beds in one of the windowless bedrooms.

"Such a fuss," Mama complained. "You'd think she was a princess, or something."

I looked up quickly. How had she guessed? To me Bessie had become the heroine of every story I ever read, and I was an avid reader.

"Please be nice to her," I begged.

"I'll be just as nice as she is," Mama snapped.

I needn't have worried. Bessie won Mama over the

minute she came through the door.

"I'm so happy Emma and I do our homework together," she said. "She knows so many answers, it takes no time at all."

Mama smiled. "Sit down. Here's a cup of cocoa and some challah I made myself."

Bessie took a bite. "Delicious," she said and gave Mama an admiring glance. Out came a platter containing cookies Mama was saving for the Sunday night visitors. "These are home-made too."

After the cookies were properly appreciated, Bessie said, "It's such a nice day. Do you think we can go to Central Park?" she asked Mama.

"It's too far to walk," I said quickly.

To my amazement, Mama fished a dime and a nickel out of the teapot. "For carfare and peanuts."

We took the horse-drawn street car to the park and in no time were feeding peanuts to the squirrels.

"Look, Emmy," Bessie pointed to a woman in a white lace dress. "What a creation she's wearing!"

Both of us loved big words, a dress was a creation; a hairdo, a coiffeur; a picture, a masterpiece; and the Equestrian Path, well, that was something which must be explored.

"See that Em?" She pointed to the sign reading Equestrian Path. "Let's go."

"But Bessie, I don't know what Equestrian means. And there's no one there."

"It says path, doesn't it. Come on."

We went. A short distance from the entrance, the path became steep and full of rocks. I wanted to go back, but she urged me on. "There's a turn. It must be better."

Suddenly we heard hoof-beats. A man and woman on

horseback galloped toward us. We scrambled to the side. We ran, we fell, we rolled out of the way. We were bruised and dirty, our Sunday best dresses were torn, but what hurt us most was the laughter of the riders echoing up and down the Equestrian Path.

I was silent on the way home and in no mood to run from the half-dozen boys who suddenly surrounded us shouting "Run, 'fraidy cat'." In front of Bessie, too!

One of them started ripping Bessie's already torn dress. How dared they! I grabbed the smallest one, about six years old and swung him into the group like a whip. The astonished would-be gangsters disappeared. Amused passers-by rescued the living whip from me.

"What a day," Bessie said.

"What a *wonderful* day," I answered. It was the day I left behind my fears; I was no longer greenhorn or 'fraidy-cat'.

School Is For Always

"TIMES ARE bad this year," Papa said. It was 1912, but times were always bad for Papa. I was nearly fourteen and graduation was a few months away. There were endless arguments between Papa and Mama about what I should do after that. I got a headache every time Papa said I wouldn't be able to go to high school.

"She's a girl. She'll get married in a few years. So why send her to high school for four years? We have Freddie to think of. A man has to work a lifetime."

Mama was furious. "So you want to take her to the shop with you because she's a girl?"

"Pearl, the baby is sick," Papa answered. "She needs doctors and medicine and cod liver oil. There just isn't money for everything. It won't be so bad. She can start as errand girl. Maybe some day she'll be forelady."

"Never!" Mama's voice was quiet, grim. She tore her one cherished possession, the diamond ring, from her finger. "This is going to the pawnbroker again. I'll get the money for business school where she'll learn to type and keep books."

Leaving public school would be a wrench; I loved that gray old building. There I could forget that I was the oldest of four, that I had to mind the baby and look out for the others. School was a haven where I could be myself. There was music and history and a whole world of geography. Even arithmetic was a challenge. It would be hard to give it up and go elsewhere, but not to go at all! Just thinking about it made my head ache. I had no desire to go to business school, but school, any school would be better than running errands.

One day, Miss Callahan, who taught English and history, asked me to remain after class. Mary Callahan, stern, gray and very thin, always wore a faded military cape. It was whispered that it had belonged to her father who was killed in the Civil War. Most of us were afraid of her, and though I couldn't think of what I had done to be kept in, my knees shook as I walked to her desk.

She gave me a rare smile and held out my history paper. "You're doing so well with everything but the dates, Emma. Why?"

"I just can't remember dates. They just don't connect well—like poetry."

"Dates are important. In a way, they do connect. They are like the hooks on which you hang your clothes. There's a time for summer clothes, a time for winter clothes, a time for children's clothes and a time for grown-up clothes. The dates of history are the hooks on which the world's events hang."

"But somehow I can't remember them."

Miss Callahan looked thoughtful. "Can you stay late several afternoons a week? I need help marking these papers."

Thereafter I helped Miss Callahan. She gave me the

class papers together with the answers. When I got through correcting some thirty-five papers, I had those dates down pat.

We became friends, Miss Callahan and I. On the afternoons I stayed late, we discussed the literature which was required reading.

"What do you think of 'The Lady of the Lake?' she asked.

"I love to read it. The words sing. But Malcolm Graeme is such a goody-goody, a sissy. Roderick should be the hero; I like battlers."

"I agree with you," Miss Callahan laughed, "though I wouldn't put it quite that way. Maybe some day you'll write a story about a battling hero. However, I think you should study law."

My head began to hurt again; I put my hands against my pounding temples.

"I can't study law. I can't even go to high school. There are four of us children, and we have nothing—nothing."

Miss Callahan wiped her spectacles. "We can only do our best. You've done it here. You'll go on, I'm sure. There are night schools. I believe school is for always."

She patted my shoulder. "I shouldn't be telling you this, but now seems the right time. You were chosen in class as valedictorian and will get the general excellence medal."

I choked a "Thank you," and dried my tears.

"And remember, school is for always."

I did.

Graduation Dress

MAMA AND Mrs. Pinsker, our next door neighbor, were arguing. I disliked Mrs. Pinsker and usually agreed with Mama. This time, however, I felt Mrs. Pinsker was right.

"Clothes are important," Mrs. Pinsker said. "You should buy a nice graduation dress for Emmy—a reward for being valedictorian. Remember the time there was so much sickness in the family, scarlet fever, measles, whooping cough? She hardly attended school that term. How terrible she felt when she was left back! Now she deserves some nice clothes."

Mama and I looked at each other. We both knew there was no money with which to buy me that 'nice graduation dress'.

"Clothes, shmoes," Mama answered bravely. "It's the people in them that are important."

"Nobody want to know anyone that looks like a beggar," Mrs. Pinsker said spitefully.

Mama's eyes blazed. "So you let your eighteen-year-old daughter go out with a married man just because he buys her clothes."

"I'm waiting till she gets a good wardrobe from him," Mrs. Pinsker answered. "Then I'll put a stop to it." She left in a huff.

Mama sighed. "I hope she doesn't come here any more. I can't stand what she's doing to Annie."

"Wasn't she going steady with Louis?"

"I asked Mrs. Pinsker about that. 'I broke it up' she answered. 'Who needs a presser? Annie can do better.'"

I was shocked by Mrs. Pinsker's treatment of Annie, but felt Mama wasn't right about clothes either. At fourteen, clothes were begining to have a meaning for me. The ill-fitting, home-made dresses made me miserable.

Mama had a bizarre color sense for that drab era; I know that she was half a century ahead of her time. When I learned that we were to wear white at graduation, I was delighted. 'You can't go far wrong with white', I thought. I didn't know what was in store for me.

"Papa brought home some white, embroidered material for your dress," Mama told me. "His boss gave it to him."

"Oh, I'm glad. Embroidered dresses are so stylish. But please buy a pattern."

"It's not necessary. The dress almost makes itself." She produced a batch of samples, none over eighteen inches long, nearly all in different designs.

I was in tears. "But Mama, this one has leaves, and this a fan design, and this one..." I got no further.

"There are plenty of samples. I'll sew them together and gather them. You'll be on the platform where the designs won't be seen. I'm so proud of you."

I wasn't to be side-tracked. "We'll be in class first. The girls..."

"Don't worry about the girls. What do they know? It's the women I'm thinking of. When the skirt is gathered—"

Suddenly a shrill voice penetrated the thin walls.

"That bitch of a daughter of yours is going out with my husband. And he the father of three kids."

"What?" Mrs. Pinsker shrieked. "You mean that bastard is married?" Then more quietly, "Come in, come in; the children too." The door slammed shut; we heard no more.

A while later, Mama was sorting some partially withered stringbeans. Mrs. Pinsker barged in. Without invitation, she seated herself at the kitchen table.

"I must tell you about that Annie of mine. She won't give that bum Max, up. Says she *lahves* him, that he'll get a divorce and marry her. 'Fool,' I told her. 'This is America. You think people can get a divorce here just by going to a rabbi?' What a lot of trouble that girl is!"

"You knew he was married. Why did you let her go out with him?"

"I didn't know for sure. Now her father will have to take care of her. With his fists, if necessary."

"*You* made all this trouble." Mama told her.

Mrs. Pinsker stormed out.

"A low woman," Mama muttered in disgust. "Clothes!"

"What did you call her?"

"A low woman," Mama repeated. "Dresses! I told you they're not important."

My graduation dress! What a horror it was. One sleeve puffed a little, the other was narrow, and the pieced flounces were crooked.

"It's not important," I kept repeating to myself and prepared for the jibes and snickers which would surely greet me.

Days later, in my grotesque white dress, I concluded the valedictory speech;

> ... "I know that we must find those
> values which are necessary for
> us, the things that really count."

I looked for Mama in the audience. Suddenly I saw her. She was beaming.

Annie? She married Louis the presser three months later.

Benny

WHENEVER I revisit the lower East Side where I was raised more than seventy-five years ago, I recall the now demolished house on Rivington Street with its rubble-filled gas-lit hallways, its peeling paint and rickety bannisters. I can almost smell the conglomeration of garlic, gefilte fish and cabbage. And I think of that terror of the building, Benny.

If anything unpleasant happened, Benny was sure to be blamed. A little girl lost her hair ribbon and a portion of her hair—Benny. A youngster fell down the stairs—he was pushed by Benny. A loose bannister—Benny. A slip on a banana peel, Benny, of course. And that monster Benny was all of five years old.

Coming home from work one evening, (I had gotten my 'working papers' at fifteen), I found Papa and Mama arguing.

"Your friend, Fanny Bushkin, doesn't know how to bring up a child," he was saying. "*I'd* teach him! He wouldn't sit down for a week."

Mama kept on koshering the meat. Carefully she

salted it on all six sides before replying. "That child has
had so many beatings, another one wouldn't make any
difference."

"I still say a good licking will knock some sense into
him. And she could keep Benny, and herself, clean. I
almost laughed in her face when she told us how her
husband washes the floor under his bed and a yard or
two around it and won't let anyone come near his part of
the room. What a filthy house she must keep!"

"Not everyone is neat," Mama retorted. "Look at the
way I have to keep picking up your cigarette butts and
clothes and papers. She hasn't been well since the baby
was born. If her husband had any heart, any decency,
he'd help her."

Papa ignored her reference to his untidiness.

"You yourself said he's the worst boy in the neighborhood. I tell you he'll grow up to be a gangster yet."

"I'm sorry I said that. No one pays any attention to him
now. Now wonder he tears the bottle from the baby. The
other day he turned the carriage over with her in it. It's
lucky she wasn't hurt."

"You forget how he throws the garbage on the steps,"
Papa answered. "Last week I nearly fell down the stairs.
And only yesterday, Mrs. Rosen caught him hacking the
bannister with a knife."

Mama made no reply. Calmly she continued salting
the meat. To her, the subject was closed. I shook my
head. "Poor little kid, I feel so sorry for him."

Going up the stairs a few days later, I found Benny
crying in the hallway. On impulse, I patted his head.
"What's the matter, Benny?"

"Papa hit me. I spill the in..." He pointed to his ink-
stained pants.

"Try to be more careful, dear," I said as I walked up the extra two flights.

The following evening Benny was waiting for me on the stairs. He pulled at my skirt.

"You touch head," he pleaded. My mouth was suddenly dry. I could hardly speak when I entered our flat.

Every night after that, Benny was there waiting for his pat on the head. One day I had some extra work and was an hour late. Benny was still on the stairs. His face lit up. "You come," he said.

I couldn't reply. I just smoothed his dark, sticky hair.

"Something should be done for that little boy," I told Mama at supper.

"What can be done?" she asked. "Mrs. Bushkin was here this afternoon, crying. She says she can't buy groceries with the two children. She's afraid he'll hurt the baby if she takes her eyes off him for a minute."

A few days later, Mrs. Bushkin solved her shopping dilemma. She locked Benny in the apartment and took the baby with her. That evening when I came home I found a group of neighbors on the stoop. I heard the names Bushkin and Benny whispered as I pushed my way through. "Busybodies," I muttered.

I walked up the stairs looking for Benny. He was not in his accustomed place in the hallway. "Are the Bushkins visiting someone?" I asked.

A muffled weeping came from the kitchen.

"What happened, Mama?"

"Benny wanted to get some cookies from the shelf over the stove. He got b-burned. He's in the hospital."

"Where was his mother?"

"She went to buy some milk and things."

"She left him alone with a lighted stove? That...that..."

"Sh—sh" Mama said. "They'll take good care of him in the hospital. His father and mother are there. They won't let anyone else see him."

I didn't insist. I was little more than a child myself. I hoped Benny would come home soon and I'd make it up to him. He died two weeks later.

This happened more than sixty-five years ago. I know now that somehow, somehow, I should have managed to see him. And whenever I hear someone talking about a bad boy, I see Benny in the dark hallway waiting for his pat on the head.

My First
'Bought' Dress

MAMA and Papa were having an argument, and it was about me!

"She's fourteen! Why can't we get working papers for her?" Papa demanded. "Look at Annie next door. Working four months, and already she brings home more than five dollars a week piecework." Papa's thin hand shook as he tugged at his bristling black beard.

"Not my Emmy," Mama shouted. "She will work in a fine office, with nice people. No sweatshop for her."

"And how will we pay the doctor and buy cod liver oil for Pearlie?" My sister Pearl was a sickly child, plagued with unending childhood diseases and a series of colds.

"We'll manage." Nervously Mama twisted the diamond ring on her finger. The ring was our sole asset, representing years of taking boarders into our overcrowded four-room walkthrough. How Mama treasured that ring, though it had semi-permanent residence in the pawnshop.

"Look at the dresses she's wearing," Papa stormed. "She can't go to high school, or even business school like that. You think you can get by with a twenty five cent remnant, and not even a pattern?"

"Oh, all right, we'll buy a pattern, though it seems foolish to spend fifteen cents for a pattern when for another ten cents we could make two dresses instead of one. Still if it must be a pattern I'll get one."

My assortment of odd dresses, with their clashing colors and unexpected bulges, had been a trial to me throughout my public school years. I sometimes complained, but not too vehemently. I understood that Mama and Papa were doing their best.

Mama won out, as usual. The diamond ring? The pawnbroker welcomed it back. Mama bought me an extra pair of shoes and the makings of three dresses. The rest of the money was hoarded for carfares and emergencies.

After passing the required examination, I was enrolled in an eighteen-month commercial course at the Hebrew Technical School for Girls. It was an excellent school providing much more than the stenography, typing, and bookkeeping I had been sent to learn. I entered a new world. There was swimming and health education and music and literature, and that combination of both, the opera. The *Ring of the Niebelungs* fascinated me. And how I loved *Leaves of Grass*, which I read aloud to my fidgeting siblings. I wept over 'Oh Captain, My Captain.'

I was not very good at the technical part of the course. Typing bothered me, the words raced ahead of my fingers. Until I learned to type one word at a time, the going was rough. But learn I did. The nagging knowledge of what it cost all of us in skimpy meals and shabby clothes spurred me on.

As graduation neared, I again felt a sense of panic. I

didn't want to leave school, but there was no help for it.

I was not quite sixteen when I got my first job. It was a one-girl office, which meant being secretary, book-keeper, file clerk and errand girl. For this I received the fabulous sum of eight dollars a week.

As was customary, I lied about my age. My boss, Mr. Abrams, winked when I said I was eighteen. Although at the time the labor laws were not strictly enforced, my claim to eighteen would save him trouble. Mr. Abrams, short, rotund, his vest stained with eggs and coffee, was proud of the fine 'Americaner' name he had given the cap manufacturing sweatshop on Bleeker Street.

"Bleeker Cap Company, on Bleeker Street yet, what could be better?" he bragged.

Bleak, bleaker, bleakest. I almost cried aloud. Was this the fine office and nice people Mama had pictured? I tried not to show my distaste for the twenty worn-out, foot-pedalled sewing machines and their equally shabby chairs. On one side was an unused table.

"See that table?" he asked. "For now, I'm a contrac-tor, but some day I'll buy my own goods, cut and finish the caps, and I won't have to beg those sons-a-bitches to help pay my wages when I run short."

The cubicle of an office, its battered desk decorated by a wedding picture of Mr. Abrams and his plump bride, was partitioned from the factory by six-foot boards, which kept out neither the thick dust nor the noise. Above the whirr of the machines, I could hear the calls for beer, the ribald jokes, the raucous laughter.

A one-girl office is a lonely place. I looked forward to the time when I went into the shop to collect the work tickets from which I figured the payroll. The eleven women and nine men were all on piecework; all that is, except Rosie. She was forelady; she apportioned the work, taught the beginners, sewed labels, and examined the finished caps. A pleasantly plump woman in her early thirties, she was popular with 'her boys and girls'. She laughed immoderately at their jokes and her slightly hoarse monotone often led the singing.

"Why don't we have lunch together in the office?" she asked one rainy day.

"I'll make the coffee," I answered eagerly. We became friends. I loved to hear the shop gossip as much as Rosie loved to tell it.

"Rachel likes Sammy, but he prefers Lillie and Lillie wants Max. That's how it is," she sighed. "Nobody is ever satisfied with what they can get."

Occasionally some coarse joke from the factory could be heard above the noise of the machines. She was amused to see me blush.

"Not good enough for you, these boys? You waiting for some sheik? Rudolph Valentino, maybe?"

"Maybe," I answered. "But meanwhile, I'm saving my lunch money and carfare for a new dress. See.." I opened my purse, "I have six dollars already."

Rosie thought a bit. "I know a manufacturer on the third floor. He makes dresses for the better stores. Maybe I can get him to sell you one wholesale."

The next lunch hour, Rosie and I went to the dress factory. Those lovely dresses! 'Would six dollars buy one?' I wondered.

Rosie finally decided I looked best in an embroidered navy blue silk. It cost eight dollars. She lent me the other two.

I could hardly wait to get home. I rushed up the stairs. Mama was making a compote. She was peeling the spotted apples and over-ripe peaches.

"Look Mama. Here's my new dress." She looked puzzled. "I saved my lunch money," I explained.

Mama was astonished. "You mean you like this plain blue dress better than the red and bright green and yellow dresses I made for you?"

I paused a long minute, then answered with an almost inaudible, "Yes, Mama."

Growing Pains

MAMA WASN'T happy about my friendship with Rosie.

"She's too old for you; you're too trusting. I'm sure she'll take advantage of you some day."

"Rosie can't be much more than thirty. And she is a good friend," I bristled. "Didn't she help me get that beautiful dress? She even lent me two dollars when I didn't have enough."

"That plain blue dress," Mama sniffed. "You look much better in the bright colored dresses I made for you."

It dawned on me that Mama was a bit jealous. I was more convinced than ever that Rosie was a good friend and would never hurt me. Every day I looked forward to twelve o'clock when Rosie came to the office to have lunch with me. I had become accustomed to the noise, the dust, the whirr of the machines and raucous laughter. Mr. Abrams was pleased with the arrangement. He gave me a dollar raise.

"I'm glad you eat lunch in. When you answer the

phone and say Bleecker Cap Company, people know I'm running a real business."

I counted the change in my purse. By coincidence, it amounted to exactly one dollar. I took the change and the extra dollar and gave it to Rosie. I apologized for the small change and thanked her for her help in buying the dress.

However, I had a bad time getting home that day. It had been a scorcher.

How I wished I had a nickel for the horse-drawn trolley. 'Why am I so thirsty?' I wondered. Then I remembered the sandwich I made for lunch. It was left-over fish which I salted and peppered to make it edible.

Those twelve blocks—they seemed endless. I felt my purse, maybe there was a penny so I could buy a small glass of 'plain'. It was empty. I was flushed and sweaty by the time I reached the shabby four-story tenement where we lived. Four flights to climb! I was nearly hysterical by the time I opened the door. I rushed to the sink and filled a glass of water. I took a few quick gulps. The glass slipped from my fingers spilling the water down my dress. How good it felt! I shrieked with laughter and emptied another on myself.

"Emmy, Emmy," my mother's frightened voice finally reached me.

"I didn't have a penny, Mama. Not one penny."

Mama took me in her arms. "It's all right, it's all right. You can keep another dollar for yourself," she added after a pause.

Although I knew that some of my former classmates were getting two and three dollars more than I was, I was afraid to leave my job. Mama depended on me to bring the money home. However, I was not to enjoy the extra dollar very long. There were disquieting rumors about the newly formed Capmakers Union and a great deal of unrest in the factory; protests about the few pennies per dozen Rosie's 'boys and girls' were getting.

One day, while Rosie and I were having lunch, Mr. Abrams stormed in.

"What do you think of those sons-a-bitches?" he stormed. "They're on the sidewalk picketing, not at their machines where they belong. You, Rosie, taught them every stitch, the ungrateful dogs. Now I'll teach them better than you did. With my fists, I'll teach them."

He dashed to the door. "Please don't go down, Mr. Abrams," I pleaded. "You might get hurt."

"Hurt me? They wouldn't dare. I'm the boss," he shouted.

But dare they did. He came limping back a few minutes later. He had been thrown to the ground when he tried to beat up some of the strikers. His lip was cut and his eyes were swollen slits.

I phoned the police but no one was arrested. The strikers proved that Mr. Abrams had started the rumpus. Two policemen were assigned to take him home.

"Serves him right," I told Rosie. "I warned him not to go." She gave me a queer look and made no reply.

The strike was still on when I came to work the following morning. Rosie and Mr. Abrams were in the office.

"So it serves me right," he shouted.

Stunned, I looked at Rosie. "You told him! I thought you were my friend."

Mr. Abrams threw an envelope on the floor near me. "There's your pay. We don't need you any more."

Tears streamed down my face as I picked up the envelope and ran out the door. Suddenly I remembered my beloved *Leaves of Grass*. I ran back. Rosie was in Mr. Abram's arms. I pointed to the picture of Mr. Abrams and his bride.

"Shame, shame," I sobbed as I snatched the book of poems. Their laughter followed me down the hallway. Suddenly I remembered Mama saying, 'Big girls don't cry'. 'I'm almost seventeen,' I told myself. I dried my tears. That day, I grew up.

1981